BARACK OBAMA

Jane Rollason

LEVEL 2

Written by: Jane Rollason

Publisher: Jacquie Bloese

Editor: Cheryl Pelteret

Designer: Dawn Wilson

Picture research: Pupak Navabpour

Photo credits:

Cover: L Downing/Reuters

Pages 4 & 5: Reuters; P Macdiarmid, S Olson, E Dunand/ Getty Images; B Marks/PA Photos.

Page 6: S Thew/Corbis.

Pages 8 & 9: Reuters.

Pages 11 & 12: AP/PA Photos; Reuters.

Pages 16 & 18: J Sullivan, L Kong/Getty Images.

Pages 20 & 21: C Somodevilla/Getty Images; Reuters.

Page 23: S Archetti/Rex Features; J Wiedel/Alamy.

Pages 24 & 25: Hulton/Getty Images; AP/PA Photos.

Pages 28 & 29: Everett/Rex Features; AP/PA Photos; Hulton/ Getty Images.

Pages 33 & 35: S Maina/Getty Images; INS/Rex Features.

Page 36: S Maina/Getty Images.

Pages 38 & 39: Reuters; M Ceneta/PA Photos.

Pages 41 & 43: AP/PA Photos; S Olson/Getty Images.

Page 44: S Ferrell/Getty Images.

Pages 46 & 47: T Sloan, C Ommanney/Getty Images.

Pages 48 & 49: F Mayer, A Gardner, Bettmann/Corbis.

Pages 50 & 51: Peter Sharkey, J Justice Jr/iStockphoto; The White House/Getty Images; Sipa/Rex Features; The White House Historical Association.

Pages 52 & 53: P Souza/The White House; B Smialowski, S Loeb/Getty Images.

Published by Scholastic Ltd. 2010

Mary Glasgow Magazines (Scholastic Ltd.)
Euston House
24 Eversholt Street
London NW1 IDB

Printed in Singapore. Reprinted in 2010.

CONTENTS

	PAGE

BARACK OBAMA

Barack and his mother, Ann Durham

Dr Barack Obama, Barack's father, born in Kenya

Barack, age 9, and his Indonesian family: Ann, her husband Lolo Soetoro and Maya, Barack's half-sister

Barack, age 18, with his grandparents, Gramps and Toot

Barack and his Kenyan family (late 80s)

Auma, Barack's sister

Barack, his wife Michelle, and their daughters, Malia and Sasha

Barack Obama, the 44th President of the United States

PLACES

Hawaii Barack was born in Hawaii in 1961.

Indonesia Barack moved here when he was six. He lived here until he was ten.

Chicago Barack lived and worked here, before he became President.

Los Angeles Barack went to university here.

Washington, D.C. The President of the USA lives here with his family at the White House.

Kenya – Barack's father's family come from Kenya.

A NEW START

'Can we change? Yes, we can!'

On January 20th, 2009, Barack Obama became the 44th President of the United States of America. He is the first African-American* to be president of the richest and strongest country in the world.

Everyone knows his face. Everyone knows his name. But who is the real Barack Obama? And where did his road to the White House start?

* An 'African-American' is a black person who was born in the USA.

CHAPTER 1
Family

'My story is only possible in America – not in any other country.'

Barack Obama's story starts in a little town in America and a village on the edge of Lake Victoria in Africa.

A mother from Kansas

Ann Dunham was born in a small town in Kansas. It was 1941. There was a world war, and the United States joined the war in the same year. Ann's father went to Europe to fight. Her mother helped to build war planes in Kansas. After the war, Ann's parents moved west all the way to Hawaii. They wanted to start a new life.

A father from Kenya

Barack's father, also called Barack Obama, was born in a small village in Kenya. He came from the Luo tribe. He helped to look after the family's animals and he went to the local school. He found school too easy because he was clever and he didn't listen.

At eighteen, Barack's father had a boring job in a shop in Nairobi. He didn't have much money. He had a wife, Kezia, with one child and another on the way. Then he met two American women. They saw how clever he was. 'Why don't you try to get a place at an American university?' they said. 'They pay for good students from Africa.'

He sent letters to thirty universities. Twenty-nine wrote back and said no. One said yes. It was the University of Hawaii. Barack arrived there as the university's first African student.

Meeting

Ann and Barack met at the University of Hawaii. It was unusual for a black man to go out with a white girl in America in those days. It was even against the law in some states. But not in Hawaii – many races lived together there. Barack and Ann married and on 4th August, 1961, they had a son. They gave him his father's African name, Barack.

Barack and his mother, Ann

Leaving

Then Harvard University offered Barack's father a place to study law. Harvard is America's most famous university, and he couldn't say no. But there wasn't enough money for Ann and their young son to go too, so they stayed in Hawaii. Ann didn't see Barack for a long time and their love died. After three years at Harvard, Barack went back to Kenya alone. He became an important man. Barack didn't see his father again until he was twelve years old.

CHAPTER 2
Indonesia

'I want to be president.'

Barack in Hawaii

Hawaii was a beautiful place for a boy to live. Young Barack loved to play in the blue sea, with the green hills behind and colourful birds in the tall trees. People of many races lived and worked there, and a person's colour wasn't important. There was only one problem for Barack – his father wasn't around. His grandparents, Gramps and Toot, and his mother, Ann, told him stories about his father, but it wasn't the same.

* * *

Then Ann fell in love with another student at the University of Hawaii. His name was Lolo Soetoro and he was from Indonesia. Lolo spent a lot of time at Barack's house. He listened to Gramps's stories for hours and he had 'play fights' with young Barack on the floor.

One day, Barack's mother had some important news. 'Lolo has asked me to marry him,' she told Barack. 'He wants to take us to his country – Indonesia.'

Indonesia! Barack was only six. He only knew Hawaii. What was this new country like?

'They've still got tigers in Indonesia,' Gramps told his grandson. It sounded like an exciting place.

✱ ✱ ✱

Ann and Barack's new world was very different from Hawaii. Most people were much poorer. Men and women worked in the fields. People washed themselves and their clothes in the wide brown river. Barack's new home was in a village in south Jakarta. Their house was small and unfinished, but it was open and cool with a fruit tree in the front. The back garden was full of animals. There were chickens and other birds, a big yellow dog, a monkey and two small crocodiles.

'There were three crocodiles,' explained Lolo, 'but one of them escaped.'

There was a man who helped in the house and with the cooking. When they arrived from the airport, he was in the garden. He had a chicken under one arm and a long knife in his other hand. He held the bird on the ground and then cut its head off. The blood was bright red in the sun. The bird stood up and ran around and around. Then the blood slowed down and the bird fell dead on the grass. For a six-year-old boy, this was a very cool new life!

Barack and his class

Barack went to the local school. He found the Indonesian language difficult, one of his teachers remembers. But she saw him as a future leader.

'He always helped his friends. He looked after the smaller ones,' she said. One day the class were writing about the future. What job did they want to do?

'I want to be president,' wrote Barack.

Barack made friends with the sons of poor families, and they ran around the streets morning and night. Sometimes bigger boys wanted to fight with him, so Lolo taught him how to fight back. Barack wrote to his grandparents and told them about his adventures. He visited them each summer too, so he didn't forget his life back in Hawaii.

Life was often hard in Indonesia. One year there was no rain and nothing grew in the fields. The next year there was too much rain and the water in the streets came up to Barack's arms. Everywhere on the streets poor people asked for money.

***

Ann wanted a good future for Barack. He was an American, and she felt that his true life was in America. But he was learning important lessons in Indonesia. He always said please and thank you. He worked hard and he didn't ask for things all the time like some American children.

Most of the American children in Jakarta went to the International School. It was too expensive for Barack's family. They had a new baby to look after now – Barack's little sister, Maya. So, five days a week, Ann woke Barack at four o'clock in the morning. She gave him breakfast but he never wanted it. Then she gave him English lessons. They studied for three hours, before he went to school and she went to work.

Barack tried different excuses. 'I'm ill,' he said, or, 'I'm too tired.'

'Well, this is no fun for me either,' Ann said.

Lolo, Ann, baby Maya and Barack

* * *

Ann wanted Barack to be a good person. She taught him about being fair. She taught him to think for himself. And she told him all about his father.

She found books for Barack on black history and Martin Luther King. She told him stories about black children from poor families in the south of America. Those children worked hard, she said, and they became important – doctors and lawyers and politicians.

But the early morning lessons and the books weren't enough. Ann wanted more for Barack. She decided to send her son back to America.

INDONESIA

Indonesia is a country of islands - it has 17,508 islands! People live on 6,000 of these islands. The main islands are Sumatra, Java and Irian Jaya.

Holland governed Indonesia for 350 years, but after World War II, it became independent. More than 300 different tribes live on the islands of Indonesia. Most people are Muslims.

Barack spent four years in Indonesia, from ages six to ten. The food was very different from the food in Hawaii. He ate dog, snake and grasshopper in Indonesia! His grandparents sent him chocolate bars from the USA.

Facts

Capital city: Jakarta, on the island of Java

Language: Indonesian

Number of people living there: More than 230 million (only China, India and the United States have more people)

Famous finds: The bones of 'Java Man' – people think he lived on Java 500,000 years ago.

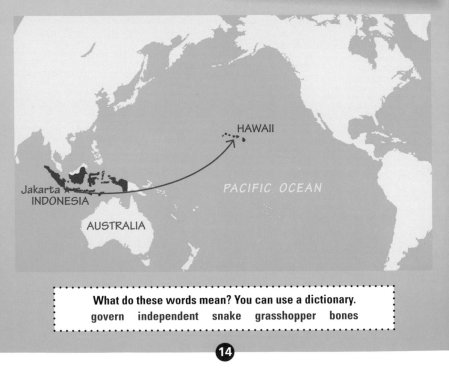

What do these words mean? You can use a dictionary.

govern   independent   snake   grasshopper   bones

CHAPTER 3
High school in Hawaii

*'When you come from Hawaii, you start to understand that
people, black or white, ... are all just Americans.'*

'It's time for you to go to back to America,' Ann said
to Barack one day. 'I'm sending you back to live with
Gramps and Toot. Maya and I will come to visit at
Christmas. Then, after about a year, we'll come back and
live there with you.'

Barack remembered Hawaii well. Each summer while
they lived in Indonesia, he visited his grandparents,
Gramps and Toot, back in Hawaii. He loved the food, the
comics and the days at the beach. Now he could enjoy
Hawaii all year round. And there were no more early
morning lessons!

Barack had a place at a top Honolulu high school called
Punahou Academy. You could see the Pacific Ocean from
the windows. But his first day did not go well. There was
only one other black pupil in the class. Later, in his book,
Dreams From My Father, Barack remembers this day.

The teacher read everyone's name out. When she read
Barack's name, the other pupils laughed. Barack wanted
to run out of the classroom, but then it got worse. The
teacher told the class that his name came from Kenya. And
she asked Barack about his family tribe. He didn't answer
for a while.

Then finally, he spoke. 'Luo,' he said.
Some boys behind him started to make monkey sounds.

'Can I touch your hair?' asked one girl at breaktime.
'Does your father eat people?' asked a boy. Questions like
this were not unusual in the 1960s in America. White and

black people did not usually live or work together in those days.

But Hawaii was different from the rest of America. The pupils came from many different races – from Polynesia, Asia and Europe, as well as America. After a few weeks, everyone lost interest in Barack's colour. He made friends and he says that he learnt to keep quiet in class. In the evenings, he read comics and listened to pop music on his radio. His new life was safe, but it was a very quiet life.

Honolulu, Hawaii

* * *

And then one day, a letter arrived from Barack's father. He was coming to visit. He was coming from Kenya for Christmas. And Barack's mother and sister were coming from Indonesia.

Barack's father knew all about his son. Ann wrote to him often and told him the family news. He knew that she was married again, with a daughter. He had another wife, too, and Barack now had five brothers and one sister living in Kenya.

The big day arrived. Barack remembers seeing his father for the first time in his grandparents' little house.

He was tall and dark, but he didn't look very strong. He wore thick glasses and had a loud laugh. He was very pleased to see Barack and he was happy because Barack was doing well in school.

Barack's father stayed for a month. It was Christmas and there were presents. Barack's father gave Barack a basketball. There was a lot of fun in the house at first but then there were arguments. Barack's father didn't want him to watch TV. He wanted him to study.

Barack's class teacher invited Barack's father to speak to her class. Teenagers often feel uncomfortable when their parents meet their friends, and Barack was the same. That day in class, Barack remembers that he felt very unhappy. He waited for the other boys to start laughing.

His father talked about the first people in the world, who lived in Kenya. He talked about different tribes and their ways of life. In some tribes a young boy still had to kill a lion before he became a man. He talked about the Luo. The older Luo men still made laws for the tribe under great old trees, he said. He told them about Kenya's fight to be free.

Barack didn't need to worry. Everyone loved his father's talk. They thought he was cool.

Barack's father was a quiet man, until someone put some Kenyan music on. When there was music, he danced. In their one month together, Barack learnt many important lessons from his father. One of those lessons was how to dance.

* * *

Over the next five years, life was good for Barack. He did well at school, he went to parties and he went out with girls. He had a part-time job at a burger bar. He joined in school activities, like singing and the school magazine, and he read a lot.

'He was very clever,' remembers one of his teachers, Eric Kusunoki.

Barack was living with his mother, Ann, and his sister, Maya. Ann and Lolo weren't married anymore, and Ann and Maya were back in Hawaii. Ann was studying at the University of Hawaii, and they had a small flat near Barack's school. Barack helped his mother with the shopping and washing, and sometimes looked after Maya. After three years, his mother's studies took her back to Indonesia. Barack didn't want to go so he moved back with Gramps and Toot. And then he discovered basketball.

Barack playing basketball

'He always had a basketball in his hands,' remembers one friend. 'He was always looking for a game.'

Barack was famous for his quick moves. The school team were good. In his last year, they won the Hawaii Schools Championship. His teammates remember that he was a good leader.

It wasn't so bad being black in Hawaii, Barack wrote later. White people didn't hate black people in Hawaii. Life in Honolulu wasn't like life on a housing project* in Harlem. They could say what they wanted. They could eat where they wanted. But he still worried about his colour and his race. His father was black, but his mother and grandparents were white. Where did he fit in a white man's world?

His friends remember him as a happy teenager. He liked to go surfing in Hawaii's famous waves and he liked to go fishing with Gramps. He loved jazz, when everyone else was listening to rock'n'roll.

His last years at high school were not easy. There were different roads he could take. He started going to lots of parties, and stopped working hard at school. He saw that luck played a big part in his friends' lives. He still couldn't answer his own question: 'Who am I?'

* 'Housing projects' are areas of houses that the government builds for poor families.

HAWAII

There are 50 states in the United States of America and Hawaii is number 50! It joined the USA on 21st August, 1959, and it was the last state to join. Barack Obama was born in the capital, Honolulu, on 4th August, 1961. 'You can't really understand Barack until you understand Hawaii,' says Barack's wife, Michelle.

Facts

Capital city: Honolulu, on Oahu Island

Languages: English, Hawaiian

Number of people living there: Nearly 1.3 million

Famous surfing beach: Waikiki on Oahu

Famous Hawaiians: Bethany Hamilton, surfer; Nicole Scherzinger (singer from The Pussycat Dolls)

It's 1,500 miles from one end of the islands to the other end. There are six main islands, and the largest island is Hawaii, also called Big Island. Hawaii has many volcanoes. The top of one volcano is as big as Manhattan Island. Kileaua Volcano on Big Island is never quiet – it is always sending fire and smoke into the sky.

In the 1800s, Westerners came to Hawaii. Americans came to grow sugar and fruit. Workers arrived from Japan, China, the Philippines and Portugal.

There are many races living in Hawaii and they respect each other. In many parts of the world, people don't always respect other races. Barack believes that the rest of the world can learn from Hawaii.

Today, Hawaii is popular for holidays! The waves can be as high as 40 feet (1.2 metres) on Hawaii's top surfing beaches.

Barack Obama held a 'Luau' – a Hawaiian party – at the White House.

What do these words mean? You can use a dictionary.
capital   island   volcano   respect

CHAPTER 4
College years

'Can words change anything?'

About a year after Barack's arrival back in Hawaii, Ann returned to Hawaii too. She was studying at Hawaii University. When Barack was at secondary school, she started worrying about him. He wasn't working hard and he wasn't doing anything with his life. 'You've lost your way,' she said to him. Barack tried not to listen to her, but he did quite well in his high school exams and he won a place at college*.

Barack as a student

In the autumn of 1979, Barack moved to Los Angeles, and started life as a student at Occidental College. There were lots of black students there. Barack liked to hang out with them. Sometimes they talked about being black, but mostly they talked about their classes, getting a good job after college and going on dates. Some black students were more political, and Barack spent time with them. He read a lot, thought a lot and people listened to his ideas. At one meeting in the college gardens, he went up to the microphone. Students were sitting on the grass. Some were playing games. He started to speak. He talked about the lives of black people in South Africa. He talked about

* Students in America go to college at age seventeen, after high school.

the need for change. The students started to listen and it felt good. But afterwards he felt unhappy. Yes, he loved making a speech. He was good at making speeches. But did he have anything to say? Can words change anything? He wasn't sure.

There was a party afterwards. He writes about it in his book, *Dreams From My Father*. He was talking to a friend, Regina. She liked his speech, she said. Another friend came over and put his arm around Barack's shoulder.

'Obama! Great party, man!' he said. 'Hey, Regina, Barack and me – we've had some good parties in our time. One weekend, we stayed up for forty hours. We started on Saturday morning and didn't stop until Monday. When the cleaners came on Monday morning, we were all sitting there. There were bottles everywhere, cigarette ends, newspapers. Those Mexican ladies started to cry,' he laughed.

'You think that's funny?' Regina said quietly to Barack. 'My grandmother was like those Mexican ladies. She had to clean up for people for most of her life. Those people probably laughed too.'

Barack knew Regina was right and he felt bad. He understood that life wasn't just about race and colour. It was about a lot of other things too.

* * *

In 1981, Barack moved to Columbia University in New York. He started to live a simpler life. He ran three miles (nearly five kilometres) a day and he didn't eat on Sundays. For the first time in years, he worked hard at his studies and he wrote a diary. He took long walks around the city. He saw the worst housing projects in black Harlem. He saw the million-dollar homes of the rich and famous on the East Side. He looked for a future among these very different lives. Where would he fit in?

Harlem, New York City

Upper East Side, New York City

Barack planned to go to Kenya and visit his father. He wanted to know him better. But then, in November, he received a phone call from a stranger. She was his Aunt Jane, she said, and she was calling from Nairobi. She had bad news. Barack's father was dead.

BLACK HISTORY IN THE USA:
SLAVERY

The history of Africans in America starts with slavery. One day in 1619 some British and Dutch pirates stopped a Portuguese ship on the Atlantic Ocean. The ship was taking slaves from Angola in south-west Africa to Veracruz in Mexico. The pirates decided to take the slaves to north America. The pirates went to Jamestown, Virginia and sold the slaves for food.

Since that day, African-Americans have fought to be equal with white people in America.

What do these words mean? You can use a dictionary.
slavery   pirate   equal   freedom   citizen

1620

White people bought and sold the first black Africans slaves in North America.

1641

America made laws about keeping slaves. The children of slave mothers always became slaves themselves, even slaves with white fathers.

1775

The campaign to end slavery started in Pennsylvania. White people in the northern states were changing their ideas about slaves. They were starting to think slavery was wrong.

1807

The government made a new law: it was against the law to bring slaves into America.

1861–5

The American Civil War was about slavery. Abraham Lincoln was president and he led the northern states (the Union). They wanted to end slavery. The southern states still wanted to use slaves. This was the worst war in American history – 650,000 Americans died. The Union army won. More than four million slaves became free.

After the civil war, many slaves were free

1865–8

Slavery ended.

1890

Slavery was against the law in the south. But new laws didn't change people's ideas. The southern states made new laws. Blacks and whites had different buses, schools, shops and workplaces. This was called 'segregation'. This was the next problem for black people.

GREYHOUND BUS DEPOT

WHITE WAITING
– ROOM –
Intrastate Passengers

Signs like this were everywhere in the south

CHAPTER 5
Chicago

'I want every child to have the chance to learn to read.'

After college, Barack took a job in a big business in New York. He had his own office and money in the bank. But he didn't want that life.

He decided to become a community worker. He knew things in America needed to change. The White House* needed to change. Government needed to change. He thought change could come from people in communities. And he wanted to help in one of those communities.

★ ★ ★

After many letters asking for a job – and very few replies – Barack finally found a job in Chicago. He arrived in Chicago in 1983 as a community worker. Chicago had its first black mayor**, Harold Washington, and the black community was full of hope.

His first job was to talk to ordinary people. He had to ask questions and listen to their answers. What worried them? What did they want to change?

There was a housing project on the South Side of Chicago called Altgeld Gardens. It was a good place to start. People there remembered when it was a happy place. Children played outside and families met in the park on holidays. But then the jobs went and a lot of the families left the area. Now the children didn't play outside. There were always groups of teenagers, doing nothing. Nobody took care of the houses. People left old cars on the streets.

* The President of the United States lives and works in the White House.
** The mayor is the leader of a city's government.

Barack worked hard. He planned meetings, he talked to people, he asked about their problems. But it wasn't easy.

Barack met a woman called Ruby. This woman was worried about her son. The week before, there was a gun fight in the street. Someone killed Ruby's son's best friend outside his own house. Barack set up a meeting. He invited church leaders, people from the area and the police chief*. But the meeting didn't go well. Only thirteen people came. The police chief didn't come. But Ruby wasn't surprised. When did anything ever change?

* * *

Barack and another worker had a new idea. They held a meeting in the street. Three of them stood on a windy street corner in late autumn. Nobody came at first. Then people slowly came out of their houses. The group on the street grew bigger until there were about twenty people.

'What problems do you talk about around your kitchen table?' they asked them. For almost an hour, people talked about the buses, the empty houses and the old cars.

Barack held more street corner meetings. Soon there were about thirty people coming every time.

* * *

The Mayor had offices ('MET' offices) to help people get jobs all around the city. There was no MET office in Altgeld, and they really needed an office! He called the head of the MET offices, Cynthia Alvarez. She agreed to come to a meeting. Barack and his helpers invited everybody and the churches helped too. A hundred people came. Ms Alvarez promised to open a MET office in the area in six months' time. And she did! Barack was beginning to see that things could really change.

* The police chief is the head of the police in the area.

BLACK HISTORY IN THE USA: SEGREGATION

Slavery ended in 1890. But life for black Americans was hard, especially in the southern states. White leaders in the southern states had a new idea: segregation. Whites had their own schools, their own churches and their own restaurants.

1955 The Montgomery Bus Protest

A black woman called Rosa Parks was sitting on a bus in Montgomery, Alabama. A white man asked for her seat. The law said: A black person must

give their seat to a white person. When Rosa Parks said no, the police took her to the police station. Black people in Montgomery were very angry. They said, 'We won't travel on the bus.' No black people travelled on the buses for 381 days. It was a protest without fighting. And it

Blacks and whites sat separately on buses

worked! After that, blacks and whites went on the same buses and they could sit anywhere. This was the start of the Civil Rights Movement, when black people fought to be equal to whites.

1963 The March on Washington

Martin Luther King Jr* led 250,000 black and white people on a march in Washington, D.C. The people on the march wanted jobs and freedom. He made a famous speech. 'I have a dream,' he told the people. He dreamed of an America where skin colour was not important.

Martin Luther King Jr

* Jr = Junior (he has the same name as his father)

1964 Civil Rights Act

Segregation because of race was now against the law. This was a very important law and the southern states had to change. It took time, but they did change.

1965 The assassination of Malcolm X

Malcolm X fought for black rights. He was the leader of the Nation of Islam and he hated white people. His real name was Malcolm Little. He changed it to Malcolm X. He said 'Little' was a slave owner's name. Many white people were frightened of him. He didn't think the Civil Rights Movement and Martin Luther King Jr were doing anything important – he thought the white people in power were controlling them. In 1965 someone from the Nation of Islam killed Malcolm X.

Malcolm X

1968

The assassination of Martin Luther King Jr.
The first African-American woman wins a seat in the US Congress.

2001

Colin Powell becomes the first African-American Secretary of State.

2004

Condoleezza Rice becomes the first African-American woman Secretary of State.

2008

Barack Obama becomes the first African-American President of the United States.

What do these words mean? You can use a dictionary.
protest   soldier   march   assassination   control   Secretary of State

29

CHAPTER 6
Finding a sister

'We didn't feel like strangers.'

Barack wanted to find out more about his Kenyan family. In 1982, he decided to write to his half-sister, Auma. Barack and Auma had the same father but different mothers. Barack's father married Auma's mother, Kezia, in 1957, when he was eighteen, and they lived in Nairobi. Barack's father was working in an office when the University of Hawaii offered him a place. He left Kezia behind and, six months later, Auma was born. It was five years before Barack's father returned to Kenya. And when he came back, he had a third wife. Auma grew up in Kenya.

Two months after writing to Auma, Barack went to meet her at Chicago airport. 'Will this be difficult?' they both were thinking before they met. But they didn't have to worry. 'We talked and talked,' Auma remembers. 'We didn't feel like strangers.'

Auma says her brother is like their father. He moves and sits the same way. He's quiet like his father, and he sits and thinks very hard. 'And we've all got the Obama hands,' she says.

Back at Barack's flat they talked for hours. Barack told Auma all about himself. She told him all about herself. She was studying in Germany. She had a nice flat and a boyfriend. But she often thought about her life and her family in Kenya. Germany and Kenya – they were two different lives.

* * *

Over the next few days, Auma told her brother all about
their father. She remembered when he came back to
Kenya, to Nairobi. He had a big house and a big car, and a
new American wife, Ruth. She and her brother Roy went
to live with him. He worked for a big American business,
and then got a government job. But then there was
trouble between President Kenyatta*'s tribe, the Kikuyus,
and the Luo. Their father said that tribes were bad for
Kenya. People were getting jobs because of their tribe, not
because they were good at the job. Kenyatta heard that
their father was a troublemaker. Things became very bad
for him. They gave him an unimportant government job.

Their father began to drink a lot. He hardly spoke
to Auma and Roy. People stopped coming to visit him
because it was too dangerous for them. His American wife
left him and then he lost his job. He moved to a terrible
house in a bad part of town with Roy and Auma. But
he still said everything was fine. Auma and Roy were
the children of Dr Barack Obama, a man who went to
Harvard – but there was no food to eat in their house. Roy
and Auma both left home when they finished school –
Roy went to America and Auma went to Germany.

After President Kenyatta died, their father got a job
again. He lived alone in a hotel room. Then he found a
young girlfriend and they had a son, George. George was
a new start for Dr Obama – he could do the right thing for
one of his children. But then he had the car accident and
he died.

Dr Obama's American son was very important to him.
'Our father talked about you so much,' Auma told Barack.
'He showed your picture to everybody. He and your mum
wrote letters, and he loved those letters. During the really

* Jomo Kenyatta was President of Kenya 1974-1978.

bad times, he read them to me.'

Before he met Auma, Barack's picture of his father came from his mother. He was a great man and Barack wanted to be like him. But this was a different picture. He wasn't a great man at all. His idea of his father was now in pieces.

Auma stayed for ten days and then flew back to Germany. As they waited for her plane, she told him about their grandfather's land in Kenya. She said it was the most beautiful place. Their grandmother still lived there. They planned a visit there together ... one day soon.

* * *

Barack worked in Chicago for three years. People in the Altgeld community knew him well. He was very busy but he felt he could do his job better. He decided to go to Havard Law School. He wanted to learn about the law, about business, about money and power. He planned to come back to Chicago after law school, and work for real change.

After three years' hard work, he needed a break. He thought about his father and his family in Kenya. He knew he had to go. What was he waiting for? Auma was teaching in Nairobi. He booked a ticket. Finally, Barack was going to find his family.

CHAPTER 7
Kenya

'I have a life in America … but a past that comes from this small piece of land in Africa.'

When Barack got off the plane in Nairobi, Auma and his Aunt Zeituni were waiting for him. They had big plans for his visit.

A market in Nairobi

The three of them drove into Nairobi in his aunt's old Volkswagen car. That afternoon, Barack and Auma visited a market in the city. They sat and watched the people go by. In his book, Barack remembers how he felt there. Nobody looked at him because he was black. His hair grew like everybody's hair. Everybody knew how to spell Obama. Nobody called him 'Alabama' or 'Yo Mama' – as they did in America. The world was black, so Barack was just Barack.

But later in a restaurant, he felt he was back in America. He and Auma sat at a table. No waiter appeared. A white

American family arrived. They sat down and the waiter took their order. The waiter set the Americans' places and brought their food. Barack and Auma were still waiting to give their order. One of the Americans asked for ketchup. The waiter brought it at once. Auma walked out of the restaurant. She was very angry.

* * *

Their next stop was Aunt Jane's. She lived in a small two-bedroom flat. Barack met Auma's mother, Kezia, and there were more aunts, cousins, nephews and nieces. There was food for everyone on the table and there were lots of questions about Hawaii, Chicago, New York. He told them he was going to Harvard, and they were happy.

Barack loved being in the centre of the large Obama family. But life was not easy for them. A few had jobs – Aunt Jane, Aunt Zeituni and Kezia – and there was food for everyone. But clothes were not new. You only visited the doctor if you were really ill. Many people slept in the two small bedrooms in Aunt Jane's flat. And there were a lot of arguments about money.

Barack learnt more about his father from his Aunt Zeituni. His father had a hard life, she told him. He was the first person from their area to study abroad. He was the first person to go on a plane. When he came back, everybody wanted his help. He was rich and important. Everybody wanted something. But when his luck changed and he lost his job, those same people forgot him. They laughed at him, she remembered. They didn't invite him to their houses. But when he was doing well again, he gave them money again.

Barack and his new family took a night train to Kisumu in the country. From there they took a bus to Barack's grandmother's land. When they arrived, more family waited to meet them. Barack sat down with Granny. He looked at the photos on the wall of her little house – photos of his grandparents, and his father as a baby. He listened to stories about his grandparents. He knew that this was not his real home. In a few weeks' time he was going back to America of course. But he felt like he was at home.

Barack and his family in Kisumu

KENYA

KENYA

Kenya has everything – high mountains, long beaches, a rainforest and a desert. It is in East Africa. Mount Kenya is the second highest mountain in Africa. Some Kenyans live very modern lives in Nairobi. Others live very traditional lives in the country, like the Maasai tribesmen.

The earliest people in the world probably lived in Kenya, two million years ago. Other people arrived there in about 2,000 BC* from all over Africa. The Kikuyu came from West Africa, and the Maasai and Luo came from southern Sudan. The Obama family are from the Luo tribe. By 800 AD**, ships were coming to Kenya from Arabia, India, Persia and China.

* BC = Before Jesus Christ
** AD = After Jesus Christ

They bought and sold many things. Then the first Europeans arrived. The Portuguese governed Kenya for 200 years, followed by the British. Barack's grandfather worked as a cook for the British army.

Kenya became independent from Britain in 1963. Jomo Kenyatta was the country's first president. Kenya became a strong, rich country, but ordinary Kenyans stayed poor. Today, most Kenyans are still poor and live on less than $1 a day. But they are all very proud of their famous son, Barack Obama.

A Maasai tribesman near Nairobi

Facts

Capital city: Nairobi

Languages: Swahili, English, tribal languages

Number of people living there: More than 38 million

Top Sport: Marathon running

Famous for: wildlife, tea

What do these words mean? You can use a dictionary.
rainforest   desert   modern   traditional   proud   marathon   wildlife

CHAPTER 8
Meeting Michelle

'I felt like the luckiest man alive.'

Barack studied at Harvard for three years. He always remembered his father's words – 'You must work hard and you must be the best. You are an Obama!' He spent most of his time with his books, and was a top student. That won him a summer job at a busy Chicago law office.

The office asked one of their new young lawyers to help him – her name was Michelle Robinson. Barack liked Michelle right away, but she wasn't so sure about him. When she first met him, she later told one newspaper, he had no money, he wore old clothes and his car was even older. He asked her out many times, and she said no many times.

But Barack didn't give up and Michelle finally agreed to spend a Saturday with him. They had lunch at a café, they walked and talked, and in the evening they went to the cinema. The evening ended with a drink at the top of Chicago's John Hancock Center.

'We clicked right away,' Michelle remembers. 'I knew I had to see him again.'

Barack invited Michelle to a community meeting in a church room with him. The people at the meeting were worried about guns in the street, money, their children's future. Barack really talked to them, she remembers, and he really listened.

'I knew he was special and that he could really understand people,' Michelle said. 'That's how I fell in love with him.'

Michelle's favourite singer is Stevie Wonder. Luckily he

was in Barack's Top 10 too. As Barack has said, 'I think it's fair to say ... I only had a chance with Michelle because I liked Stevie Wonder too.'

* * *

Two years later, Barack took Michelle out for a meal one evening. When the coffee and chocolates arrived, Barack asked Michelle to marry him. She was very surprised. But she said yes.

Barack took Michelle back to Hawaii to meet his family. He writes about the meeting in his book. Gramps and Toot loved her, he says.

'She's quite a looker!' Gramps said to Barack.

'She's a very sensible girl.' For Toot, that was much more important than good looks.

Barack and Michelle, October, 1992

Barack then took Michelle to Kenya to meet his other family. They loved her too, especially because she knew more words in Luo than Barack. Barack and Michelle married in Chicago in October, 1992, in front of their families from Chicago, Hawaii and Kenya. They danced to 'You and I' by Stevie Wonder.

Michelle Obama

Michelle Robinson was born in 1964 in Chicago. She and her older brother Craig grew up in a one-bedroom flat on the South Side, a mainly black part of the city. Both her parents worked. Michelle says they were 'a good hard-working family. We always had dinner together around the table.'

The Robinson family can follow their history back to slave times. Michelle's great-great-grandfather was a slave in South Carolina. Some of the Robinson family still live there.

Michelle and her brother Craig did well at school. They got top marks and both went to university. Craig became a basketball coach at Oregon State University. Michelle studied sociology and African-American studies at Princeton, before going on to study law at Harvard. After working at the Chicago law office, she moved to the Mayor's office. Later, she worked for the University of Chicago.

Everyone wants to know where Michelle goes shopping. Many people love her clothes and she has appeared on the front of *Vogue* magazine. Read any list of the world's best-dressed women, and Michelle's name is always there!

What do these words mean? You can use a dictionary.
coach   sociology

CHAPTER 9
Campaigning in Chicago

'Change won't come from the top. It will come from the work we do with the community.'

After Harvard, Barack went back to Chicago to his job as a community worker. Life on the South Side was worse. More houses were falling down and more teenagers were in trouble. Families with enough money were moving away from the area. African-American voters wanted politicians to listen to them.

In 1993, Barack took a job as a lawyer. He worked with ordinary people and their problems. Michelle changed jobs too, and started work for the Mayor's office.

Over the next two years, Barack wrote his first book, *Dreams From My Father*. He was going to write a book about his work in Chicago, but he found himself writing about his life – and his family. Not many people bought it, but he enjoyed writing it.

Barack still wanted to change things for people like Ruby in Altgeld Gardens. He knew now that change mainly came from the top. The people with the real power were the politicians. Barack decided to join them.

In 1997, while he was campaigning for changes to the law, terrible news came from Hawaii. His mother had died, and he was thousands of miles away. It was the greatest sadness of his life, he said afterwards.

Barack campaigned hard. He talked to anyone who stopped to listen. He went to hundreds of meetings, to shops and churches. When he saw two men standing on a corner, he crossed the street to talk to them. He won his first election in 1997 and he became a senator* in the Illinois State Senate.

Barack at work

In 1998, Barack and Michelle became parents when their daughter, Malia Ann, was born on 4th July, Independence Day. In the election of that year, he won his seat in the Senate for four more years.

Barack worked hard at his job in the Illinois Senate. He spent family time with his wife and daughter. He exercised, read books and slowed down for a while. The next year, on 7th June, Michelle and Barack's second daughter, Sasha, was born.

In 2009, Barack wrote a letter to his daughters. He said, 'When I was a young man, I thought life was all about me. But then you two came into my world ... with those smiles that light up my day. And suddenly, all my big plans for myself didn't seem so important anymore ...'.

* See page 44 ('How the government works')

CHAPTER 10
To the White House

'People of the world ...This is our moment. This is our time!'

People in the world of politics were beginning to notice Barack. They were starting to talk about a new voice and a new face in the Democratic Party. 'Could this be a future president?' they were asking. Barack worked hard as state senator. Between 2000 and 2004, he pushed through 800 laws. And in 2004 he became a candidate for the United States Senate.

For his campaign, Barack had a new line: 'Yes, we can.' He was ready to fight and to win. But campaigning for the senate meant being away from home for days at a time. When Michelle was reading a bedtime story to Malia and Sasha, Barack was sitting in a cold meeting room somewhere in Illinois. He travelled miles around the state. Sometimes, after hours of driving, he found three people waiting around a kitchen table. But he always listened. People talked about their jobs, their businesses, their children's school, their parents, their pets. They were mostly too tired and too busy to care about politics or President Bush or Democrats.

That year, 2004, America was voting for the President. Barack made a big speech to the Democratic Party. It was on live television around the world. Barack spoke about his mother and father, and told his own story. He wanted America to hope. Everyone loved the speech and Barack was famous.

In January, 2005, Barack Obama became only the fifth African-American to win a seat in the US Senate. He quickly learnt two things. First, Washington politics

HOW THE GOVERNMENT WORKS

The United States is a republic (it has a president, not a king or queen) and a democracy – the American people vote for their president. Every American over the age of 18 can vote. The president leads the government.

There are three parts to the US government. They all control each other.

THE PRESIDENT

⭐ runs the country.

⭐ talks to leaders of other countries.

⭐ chooses the people who help him with his work.

⭐ is head of America's armed forces.

⭐ lives and works in the White House.

⭐ chooses the judges in the Supreme Court.

⭐ tells Congress what he wants to do.

THE SUPREME COURT

The Supreme Court judges have to decide things. They are like the referees at a football match.

The Supreme Court does not allow the President and Congress to do anything against the law.

CONGRESS

Congress makes new laws. There are politicians from the two main political parties in Congress – the Democrats and the Republicans. Congress includes the Senate. There are 100 people in the Senate – two for each state in America. They are the State Senators. Barack Obama was State Senator for Illinois, before he became president.

:::
What do these words mean? You can use a dictionary.
control   armed forces   judge   referee   make sure
:::

wasn't about ordinary people and their lives. Second, the government and the country were not working together. Barack's politics were different – he liked to work with politicians from other parties, not against them. He wanted to change things for ordinary people. He wanted to find ways for hard-working families to pay less money to the government, and he wanted better schools.

In 2006, Barack wrote his second book, *The Audacity of Hope*. This time, he wrote about his ideas for the future of politics in the USA, and the world. The book went to Number 1 in the *New York Times* Top Ten books. He travelled to bookshops around the country – thousands of people waited in line at each bookshop. He was more like a Hollywood film star than a politician. Everyone asked him the same question: 'Why don't you think about being the next President?'

One evening, Barack talked to Michelle about it.

'What do you think?' he asked her.

'OK,' she said, 'but you must do one thing for me.'

'What's that?' he asked.

'You must stop smoking!'

* * *

So Barack became a candidate for president of the United States.

Barack has always listened to ordinary people. He knows what they care about. And his campaign was about them. His campaign sent them a message of hope.

'Can we change things?' he asked. 'Yes, we can,' he answered.

Election day was November 4th, 2008. Barack started the day by playing basketball. 'It always brings me good luck,' he says. When voting closed, the world waited for the result. 'White Americans won't really vote for a black president,' people said. But they did! Barack won 53% of all the votes – he was President!

Barack Obama became the 44th President of the United States, and the first African-American president. On 18th January, 2009, Beyoncé, Bruce Springsteen and will.i.am all played at a big party in Washington, D.C. for the event. The next day was Martin Luther King Day. Barack asked Americans to spend the day working for their community for free. On 20th January, Obama became the new president. It was a cold winter's day, but nearly two million people stood outside at the White House in Washington, D.C. to watch. Millions of people watched it around the world. That evening Barack and Michelle went to ten different parties!

On 21st January, the new president's work began.

TECHNO PRESIDENT

Barack was the first politician to use new technology to win an election. He never goes anywhere without his BlackBerry. He uses an Apple Mac laptop. He has a website called barackobama.com.

His team used the Internet to talk to voters all over the USA. Ordinary people felt they were part of Obama's campaign. Barack talked to voters by email, on his blog and in text messages.

100,000 people joined his Facebook group in its first nine days. By the time he started his campaign on 11th February 2008, 250,000 people belonged to his Facebook group.

John McCain, the Republican candidate for president, made a big mistake. He said he didn't know anything about computers! That worried a lot of voters.

What's on the President's iPod?

Bob Dylan, Jay-Z,

Sheryl Crow,

Bruce Springsteen,

Michael Jackson,

Yo-Yo Ma and

Stevie Wonder.

> **What do these words mean? You can use a dictionary.**
> technology   blog

FAMOUS PRESIDENTS

There were 43 presidents of the USA before Barack Obama. Read about three of the most famous US presidents. They all had new ideas and they all had to make difficult decisions.

1st George Washington 1789-97

George Washington owned land in Virginia. Britain governed America

in those days. Washington and other landowners wanted independence from Britain, and in 1775 they went to

war. The Americans won the war, and on 30th April, 1789, George Washington became the first President of the USA. He died in 1799. His picture is on the US$1 banknote.

The American War of Independence: Washington led the American army in the fight against the British government from 1775 – 1782.

The Constitution: Washington helped to write America's Constitution. This tells us the laws and rights of the American people. America still uses it today.

Washington, D.C.: Washington chose an area for the home of the US government – it was named after him and it is still the home of government today.

16th Abraham Lincoln 1861-5

Abraham Lincoln's family was poor, but Abraham wanted to learn.

He became a lawyer and then a politician. He wanted to stop slavery in the Southern states and when he was President, he

fought the South in the American Civil War. A civil war is a war between two sides of the same country.
In 1865 a man from the South killed Lincoln. Lincoln's picture is on the US$5 banknote.

The End of Slavery: Lincoln changed the law on slavery. Slavery ended in the United States in 1863.

The American Civil War: Lincoln led the North in the Civil War against the South. The South wanted to keep slaves and they wanted independence from the North. 600,000 people died in this war.

The 'Gettysburg Address': There was terrible fighting at Gettysburg, Pennsylvania, during the Civil War. After the war, Lincoln made a famous speech there. The dead did not die for nothing, he said. They died for people to be free.

Fighting at Gettysburg

Who is or was the most famous leader of your country?
What are they famous for?

John F. Kennedy was the youngest president in US history. He was only 43 years old. He was young and full of new ideas, and people called him 'JFK'. They also loved his beautiful and clever wife, Jackie Kennedy. JFK wanted to make big changes to civil rights and to help the poor, but someone killed him in 1963.

Famous Speech: 'Don't ask what your country can do for you,' said JFK when he became President, 'ask what *you* can do for your country.'

The Vietnam War: The Vietnam War started before JFK became President. But he sent more money and men to the war to stop the Communists in North Vietnam. The war did not end until 1975, and millions of people died, including 60,000 Americans.

First Man on the Moon: JFK started the programme to send a man to the moon in 1961. Neil Armstrong landed on the moon in 1969, eight years later.

What do these words mean? You can use a dictionary.
decisions   independence   slavery   rights   Communists   programme   moon

Inside the

The White House has been home to every US president since 1797. Today the White House is a museum, a very busy office, a private home and a symbol of America. Lots of different people – from Heads of State to schoolchildren – come here to visit the First Family. (The President's wife is the First Lady; their family is the First Family.)

The White House has 132 rooms on 6 floors. There are 35 bedrooms.

THE WEST WING: This is the centre of power – the President's offices are here.

The Oval Office: When you think of the President of the United States, you probably think of him sitting at a desk in this office. In 1909, the famous Oval Office opened. Barack Obama doesn't use it much – he has a smaller, more comfortable office next door.

The State Dining Room: The President can invite up to 140 guests to dinner in this large dining room.

The Tennis Court: Barack Obama is a great basketball player. White House staff have turned the tennis court into a basketball court, so the President can practise.

White House

Imagine you are Malia or Sasha. What is it like being a teenager in the White House? Where do you hang out? Do you bring your friends home?

TOP TWO FLOORS: The home apartments are private. Barack, Michelle, their daughters and Bo the dog live here.

THE EAST WING: The First Lady usually runs her busy life from here.

The Family Cinema: There are 40 comfortable red seats in the White House cinema. Sometimes presidents practise their speeches here. More often the First Family and their guests watch films here. Many new Hollywood films come to the White House before they open in cinemas.

Lincoln's Bedroom: If anyone invites you to stay at the White House, ask to stay in this room! Abraham Lincoln used it as his study, but he never slept in here. It has a very big bed in it and a copy of his Gettysburg speech (see p. 49). Today it's a guest bedroom.

The Vegetable Garden: Michelle Obama made this new garden. Fruit and vegetables from here go to the White House kitchens and they make food for people living on the streets.

What do these words mean? You can use a dictionary.
Heads of State   slave   private   symbol   court

A Day in the Life of

Barack Obama has the most famous job in the world – he's President of the United States! But what does he do every day? Let's look at a day in his life.

6.30

Barack and Michelle start their day with exercise in their gym, followed by a family breakfast. After Malia and Sasha leave for school, the President spends 45 minutes reading government papers and looking at the day's newspapers.

9.00

In the Oval Office, the President makes phone calls to other leaders, like the German Chancellor or the Russian Prime Minister.

Barack receives thousands of letters and e-mails from ordinary Americans. Each day he answers ten letters. He wants to understand ordinary people's hopes and worries.

9.30

Every day there are meetings about the country's safety, the economy and the most important things happening in the world and in the United States.

11.00

There is a meeting in the East Room. It is about the safety of America's computers. The President speaks to people at the meeting and answers questions.

12.00

The President is on his way to a meeting across town. But it's lunchtime and he's hungry. He stops his big black car at one of his favourite hamburger restaurants, Five Guys. There are some people sitting at a table outside. The President says hello on his way in – they can't believe it!

President Obama

13.00

The meeting across town is about the weather. In 2005, a terrible hurricane called Katrina killed more than 1800 people in the southern city of New Orleans. The President doesn't want this to happen again. He wants to know if the south is ready for this year's hurricanes.

14.00

The President makes more phone calls to leaders in other countries. Then he meets newspaper writers in the East Room. When he says something important, it appears online within minutes and on the TV and radio news that evening.

16.30

The President gets a haircut. Zariff has cut Barack's hair since 1992, when Barack still lived in Chicago. Barack pays $21, the same as he always has (and the price of a plane ticket from Chicago to Washington).

17.00

The President discusses new plans with his team.

18.30

Barack takes a break. He goes upstairs to the Home Floor. The First Family eat dinner together and hang out. He helps the girls with their homework. But he still has his Blackberry in his pocket!

20.00

There are more government papers to read and more decisions to make.

21.30

The President takes Bo out for his evening walk across the White House garden.

22.00

Barack goes into his study on the Home Floor. This is his quiet time, when he can read and think.

What do these words mean?
You can use a dictionary.
gym   Chancellor   Prime Minister
hurricane   economy

Would you like to live the President's life? Why? Why not?

CHAPTERS 1–3

Before you read

Use a dictionary for this section.

1 Use these words to answer the questions.

argument   race   surfing   tribe   war

  a) Which one is a sport?

  b) Which one can happen when two people do not agree?

  c) Which one is a fight between two countries?

  d) Which one is a group of people from an area with the same language?

  e) Which one shows the group of people you belong to?

2 Look at 'People and Places' on pages 4–5. Find these places.

  a) Barack's father's family come from here.

  b) Barack studied here.

  c) Barack was born here.

  d) The White House is here.

  e) Barack lived and worked here.

3 What do you know about Barack Obama? Think of three things.

After you read

4 Answer these questions.

  a) Where did Barack's parents meet?

  b) Why didn't Ann and Barack go with Barack's father to Harvard?

  c) Who was Ann's second husband?

  d) What animal did Lolo's cook kill on Barack's first day in Indonesia?

  e) Why did Ann wake Barack at 4 am on schooldays?

  f) Why did Barack feel unhappy on his first day at school in Hawaii?

  g) Why were there arguments when Barack's father came to stay?

5 As a teenager, Barack went surfing and fishing, wrote for the school magazine, listened to jazz, played basketball and read a lot. How are his teenage years the same as or different from yours?

CHAPTERS 4-6

Before you read

6   Choose the best word to complete these sentences:

campaign   community   history   law   power   speech   state

a) ... tells us about the past.

b) There are 50 ... in the USA.

c) A ... says if something is right or wrong.

d) The head teacher usually makes a ... at the end of the school year.

e) If you want the ... to change people's lives, become a politician!

f) Some teenagers have started a ... to change the voting age to 16.

g) A ... is a group of people who live in the same area.

7   When Barack was a child, he lived in Hawaii and Jakarta. Then he went on to college in California. What are the good things about moving from one country to another? What are the bad things?

After you read

8   Are these sentences true or false? Correct the false sentences.

a) At college in Los Angeles, Barack and his friends talked mostly about being black.

b) Barack didn't like making speeches.

c) He changed his lifestyle when he moved to New York.

d) He knew he wanted to work in black Harlem.

e) It wasn't easy to find a job as a community worker.

f) Nothing changed in Altgeld Gardens when Barack was working there.

g) Barack and Auma have the same mother but different fathers.

h) After President Kenyatta died, things became better for Barack's father.

i) After five years in Chicago, Barack decided to visit Kenya.

9   Barack has a lot of family in Kenya. He doesn't see them very often. Do you have family in another part of the world? Do they feel like family or more like strangers?

CHAPTERS 7–10

Before you read

10 Answer these questions.

   a) Who did Barack learn good things about his father from?

   b) Barack's father grew up in the village of Kisumu. Who still lived there when Barack first visited?

   c) Who looked after Barack when he started a summer job at a Chicago law office?

   d) What did Gramps and Toot think of Michelle?

   e) What did Barack say was the greatest sadness of his life?

11 Put these words in the poster:

   candidate   election   party   vote

> ## SHOW THE POLITICIANS WHAT YOU THINK
> **OCTOBER 4th IS a)... DAY**
> **Your b)... can make a difference!**
> **There are three c)... – one from each of the main political d)....**
> **Don't forget – 8th October! Be there!**

After you read

12 Put these events in the right order.

   a) Barack and Michelle moved into the White House.

   b) Barack pushed through 800 new laws in the Illinois Senate.

   c) He became a candidate for president.

   d) He became a United States senator.

   e) He decided to run for president.

   f) He made a big speech to the Democratic Party.

   g) His second book came out.

   h) The American people voted for Barack Obama as President.

13 Why are these things important in Barack's story?
   * a chicken * Mexican cleaners * a surprise phone call from Aunt Jane * a Volkswagen car * Stevie Wonder * 4th November, 2008